That's My Dog!

I HAVE A PUG

I0799027

By Benjamin Proudfit

Gareth Stevens
PUBLISHING

Please visit our website, www.garethstevens.com. For a free color catalog of all our high-quality books, call toll free 1-800-542-2595 or fax 1-877-542-2596.

Library of Congress Cataloging-in-Publication Data
Names: Proudfit, Benjamin author
Title: I have a pug / Benjamin Proudfit.
Description: Buffalo, New York : Gareth Stevens Publishing, [2026] | Series: That's my dog! | Includes index | Audience term: Juvenile
Identifiers: LCCN 2024034462 | ISBN 9781482470062 (ebook) | ISBN 9781482470048 (paperback) | ISBN 9781482470055 (library binding)
Subjects: LCSH: Pug–Juvenile literature. | Pets–Juvenile literature.
Classification: LCC SF429.P9 P76 2026 | DDC 636.76–dc23
LC record available at https://lccn.loc.gov/2024034462

First Edition

Published in 2026 by
Gareth Stevens Publishing
2544 Clinton Street
Buffalo, NY 14224

Copyright © 2026 Gareth Stevens Publishing

Editor: Kristen Nelson
Designer: Leslie Taylor

Photo credits: Cover, p. 1 Kanyshev Andrey/Shutterstock.com; p. 5, 23 Serhiy Kobyakov/Shutterstock.com; p. 7, 24 (puppy) Ezzolo/Shutterstock.com; p. 9, 24 (wrinkles) Eric Isselee/Shutterstock.com; p. 11, 24 (fur) HelenWalkerz65/iStockphoto.com; p. 13 Yekatseryna Netuk/Shutterstock.com; p. 15 Kanyshev Andrey/Shutterstock.com; p. 17 New Africa/Shutterstock.com; p. 19 Khakimullin Aleksandr/Shutterstock.com; p. 21 fongleon356/Shutterstock.com.

All rights reserved. No part of this book may be reproduced in any form without permission in writing from the publisher, except by a reviewer.

Printed in China

Some of the images in this book illustrate individuals who are models. The depictions do not imply actual situations or events.

CPSIA compliance information: Batch #QS26GS: For further information contact Gareth Stevens, New York, New York at 1-800-542-2595.

Find us on

Contents

This is my dog.

His name is Pogo.

He is a pug.

We got Pogo when
he was a puppy.
A puppy is a baby dog.

Pugs are small dogs.
They have flat faces.
They have wrinkles.

They have short coats.
They can be black.
They can be light brown.

Pugs shed a lot.
This means they
lose their fur.
I brush Pogo every day!

Pogo takes short walks.
He gets tired fast!

Pogo lays inside
on hot days.
Pugs need to stay cool.

They like to play
with their family.

They like to sleep too.

My dog is the best.
I love my pug!

Words to Know

fur

puppy

wrinkles

Index